Fables & Folktales

The Monkey King

by Tyler Gieseke

Dash!
LEVELED READERS
An Imprint of Abdo Zoom • abdobooks.com

Level 1 – Beginning
Short and simple sentences with familiar words or patterns for children who are beginning to understand how letters and sounds go together.

Level 2 – Emerging
Longer words and sentences with more complex language patterns for readers who are practicing common words and letter sounds.

Level 3 – Transitional
More developed language and vocabulary for readers who are becoming more independent.

abdobooks.com

Published by Abdo Zoom, a division of ABDO, PO Box 398166, Minneapolis, Minnesota 55439.

Dash!™ is a trademark and logo of Abdo Zoom.

Printed in the United States of America, North Mankato, Minnesota.
102025
012026

Photo Credits: Adobe Stock, Artistly, Flickr, Shutterstock, ©Louis Davilla Wiyono p.cover/ CC BY-NC-SA 2.0
Production Contributors: Jennie Forsberg, Grace Hansen, Tyler Gieseke
Design Contributors: Candice Keimig, Neil Klinepier, Colleen McLaren

Library of Congress Control Number: 2025936787

Publisher's Cataloging in Publication Data

Names: Gieseke, Tyler, author.
Title: The monkey king / by Tyler Gieseke
Description: Minneapolis, Minnesota : Abdo Zoom, 2026 | Series: Fables & folktales | Includes online resources and index.
Identifiers: ISBN 9798384940050 (lib. bdg.) | ISBN 9798384940814 (ebook) | ISBN 9798384941194 (read-to-me ebook)
Subjects: LCSH: Monkey King (Fictitious character)--Juvenile literature. | Folk literature, Chinese--Juvenile literature. | Monkeys--Juvenile literature. | Enlightenment--Juvenile literature. | Conduct of life--Juvenile literature. | Intellect of animals--Juvenile literature. | Cultural identity--Juvenile literature. | Fables--Juvenile literature.
Classification: DDC 398.2 [E]--dc23

Table of Contents

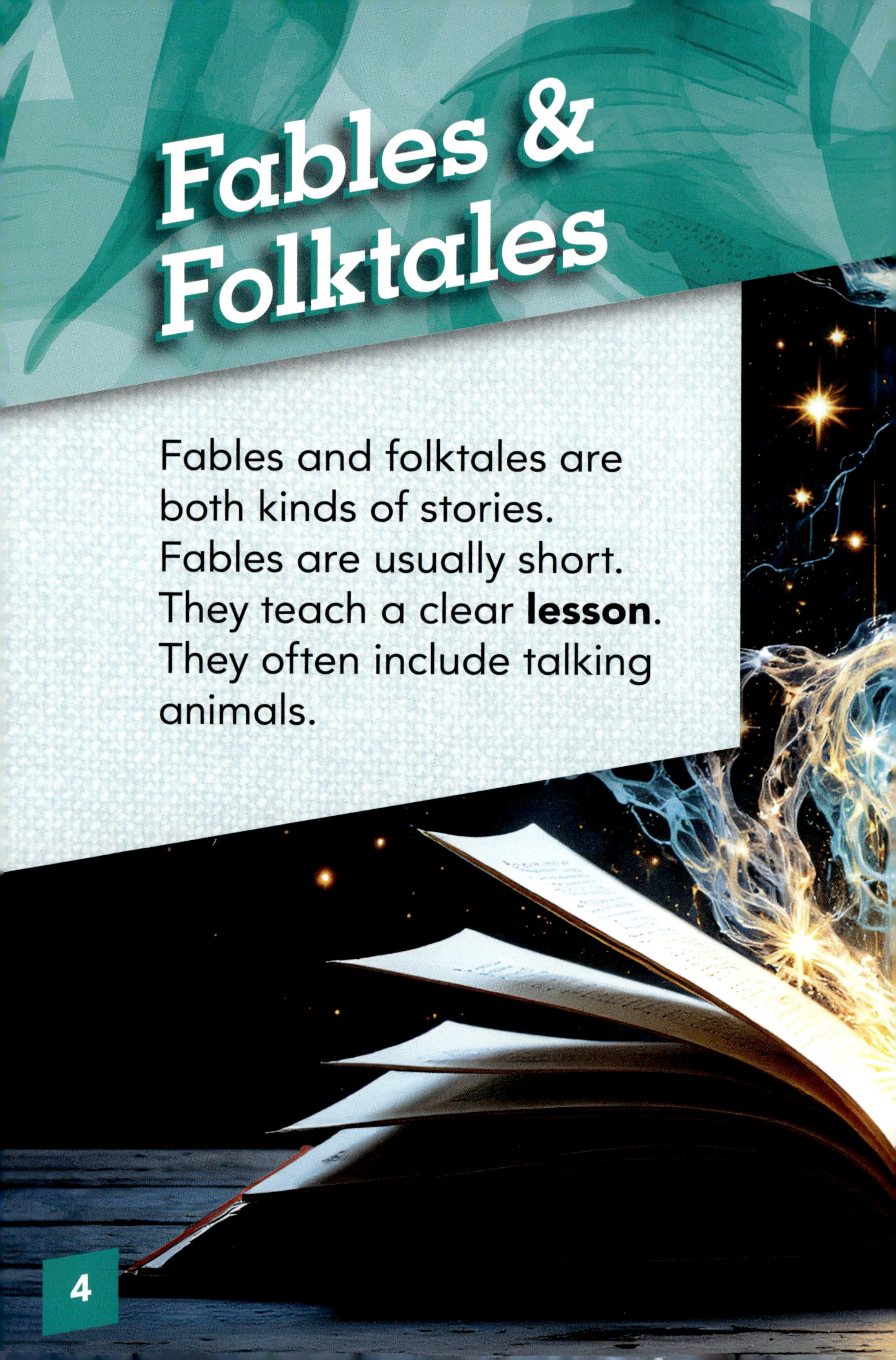

Fables & Folktales

Fables and folktales are both kinds of stories. Fables are usually short. They teach a clear **lesson**. They often include talking animals.

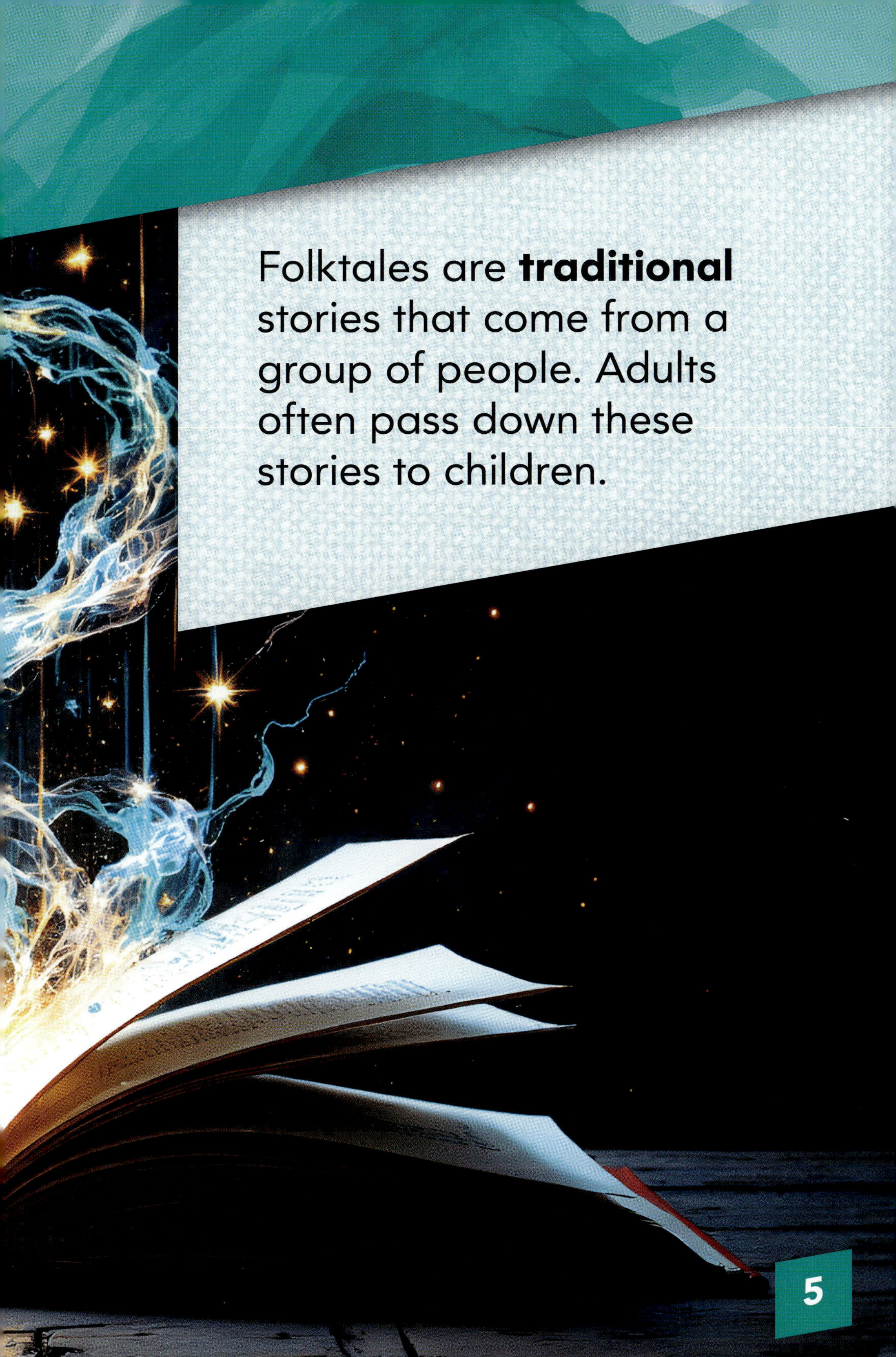

Folktales are **traditional** stories that come from a group of people. Adults often pass down these stories to children.

The Monkey King

One folktale from China tells of a monkey who became powerful enough to take on the king of heaven! The monkey was born from a magic stone on a mountain. He showed bravery one day by jumping through a waterfall. So, the other monkeys named him their king. The Monkey King grew in power. He used his power to escape **reincarnation**.

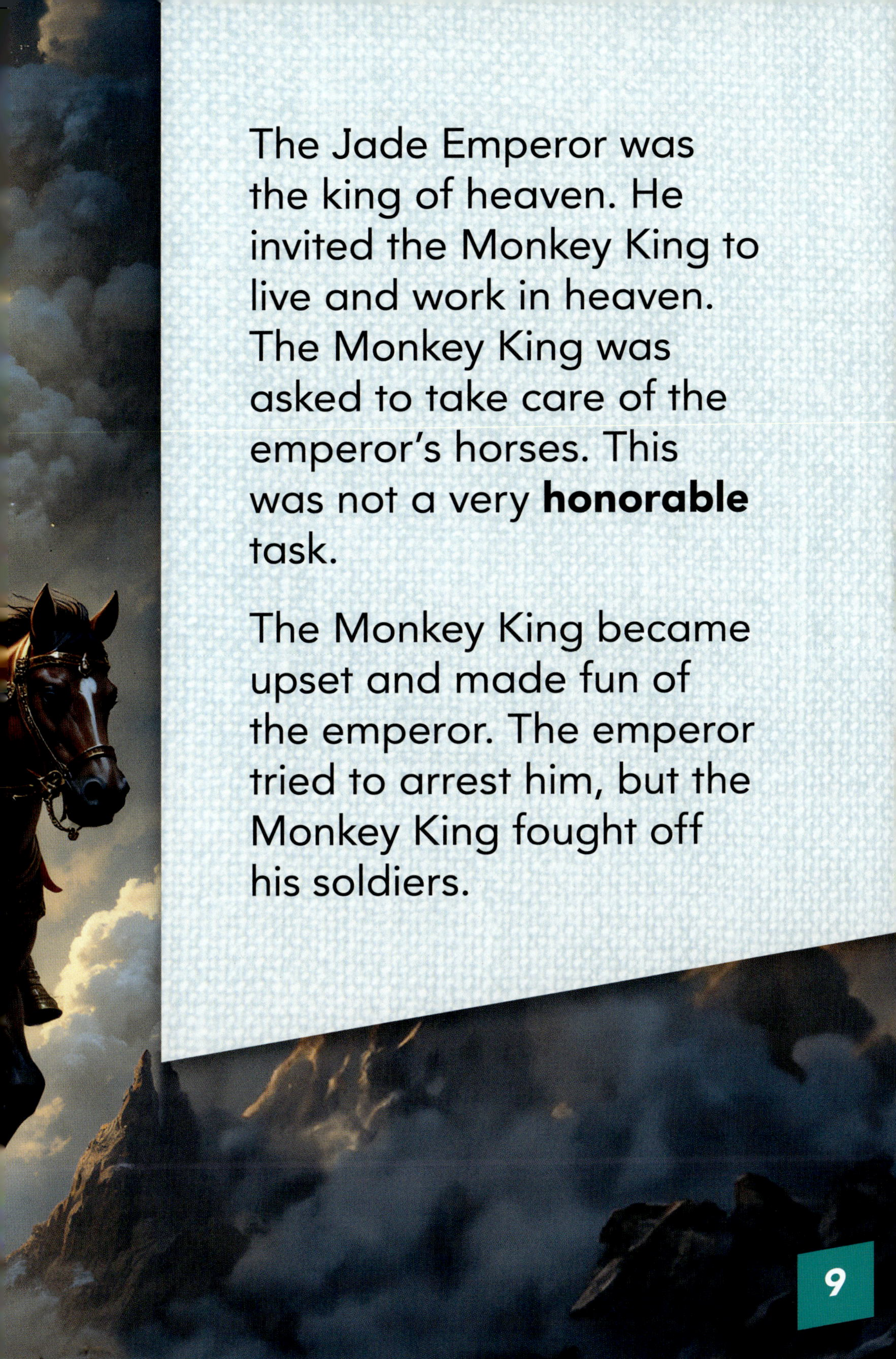

The Jade Emperor was the king of heaven. He invited the Monkey King to live and work in heaven. The Monkey King was asked to take care of the emperor's horses. This was not a very **honorable** task.

The Monkey King became upset and made fun of the emperor. The emperor tried to arrest him, but the Monkey King fought off his soldiers.

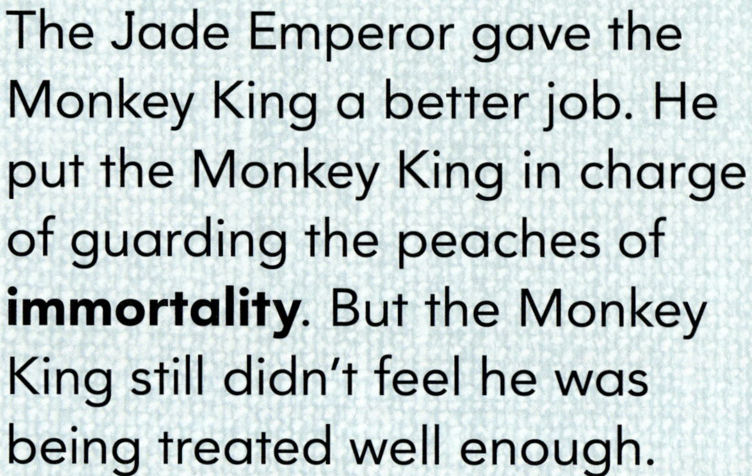

The Jade Emperor gave the Monkey King a better job. He put the Monkey King in charge of guarding the peaches of **immortality**. But the Monkey King still didn't feel he was being treated well enough.

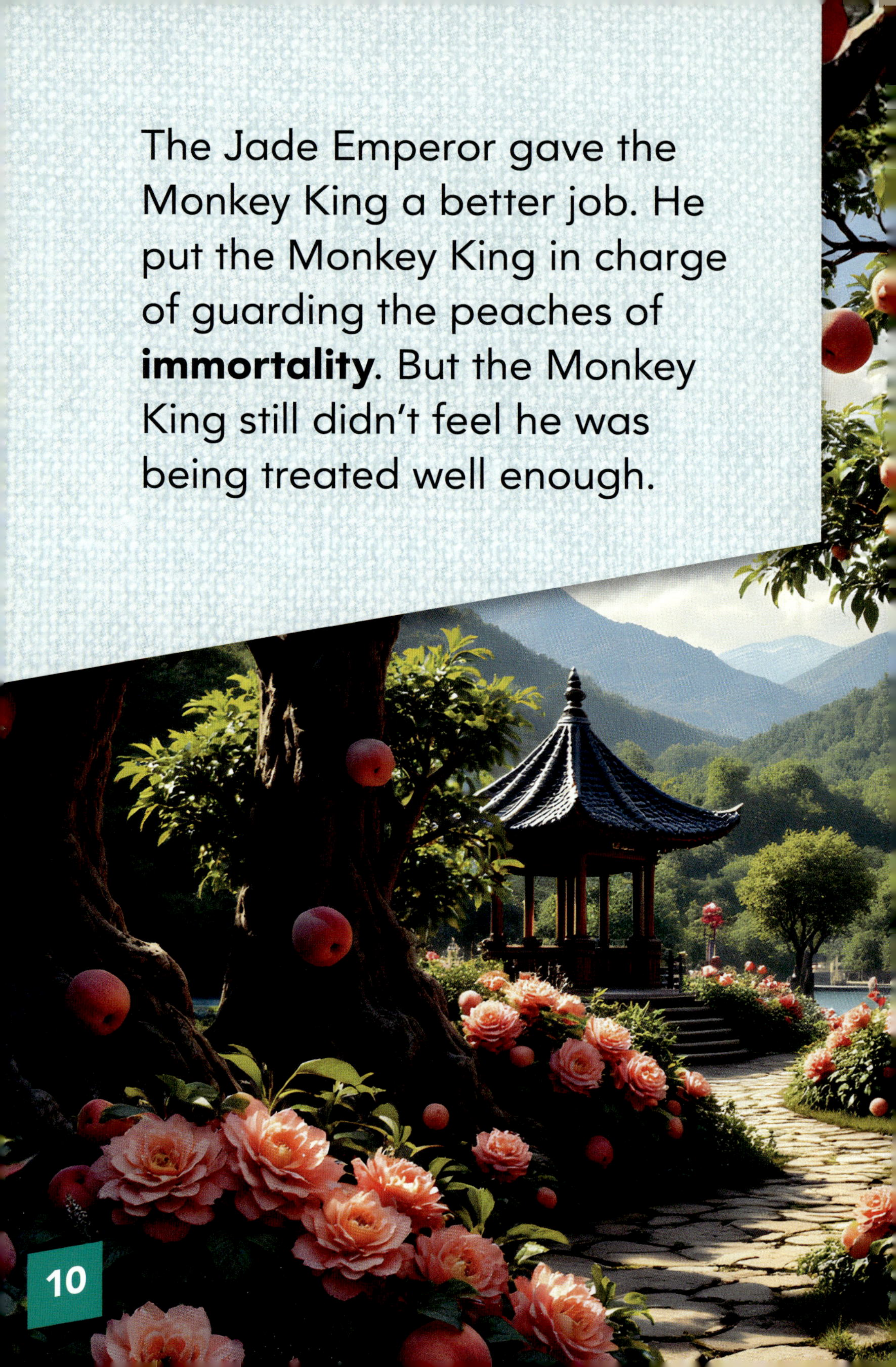

So, he ate all the peaches in the garden. The Jade Emperor asked Buddha to help. Buddha trapped the Monkey King under a mountain!

The Monkey King was stuck under the mountain for 500 years. Then a **monk** found him and offered to help. But the monk made the Monkey King agree to behave better and become one of the monk's followers.

The monk taught the Monkey King to let go of his anger and **jealousy**. The Monkey King grew in wisdom and even achieved **enlightenment**.

Lessons

A folktale often goes beyond the story itself to teach powerful **lessons**. One lesson from the Monkey King is that it's important to be happy with one's place in life. The Monkey King was a powerful ruler, but that wasn't enough for him. He wanted to be a god! This only caused confusion and fighting.

It's important to know the limits of your power and to be happy with those. For example, you don't have the power to tell your teacher or your parents what to do. But you can always speak up and say what you think. Let that be enough.

Another **lesson** from the Monkey King is that improvement is always possible. In the folktale, the Monkey King makes choices that are so poor he ends up trapped under a mountain. Still, he learns to do better.

Let's say you've had a rough week where you haven't gotten along with your brothers and sisters. You might feel like things will never get better. But they can. You just have to start somewhere—perhaps by agreeing to do better, like the Monkey King did.

More Facts

- The Monkey King has special powers. One is the ability to change his shape into 72 different things, including weapons and animals.
- The story of the Monkey King comes from the famous Chinese novel *Journey to the West*, published in the 1500s.
- The 2023 Netflix film *The Monkey King* was based off this Chinese folktale.
- The Monkey King has also appeared in TV shows and video games.

Glossary

enlightenment – the goal of some religions, when someone no longer suffers.

honorable – respected.

immortality – unending life.

jealousy – anger at someone who has what you want.

lesson – a teaching, or something learned.

monk – a man living a religious life.

reincarnation – the cycle of being reborn into a new body after death.

traditional – describing something done regularly and over time by a group of people.

Index

Online Resources

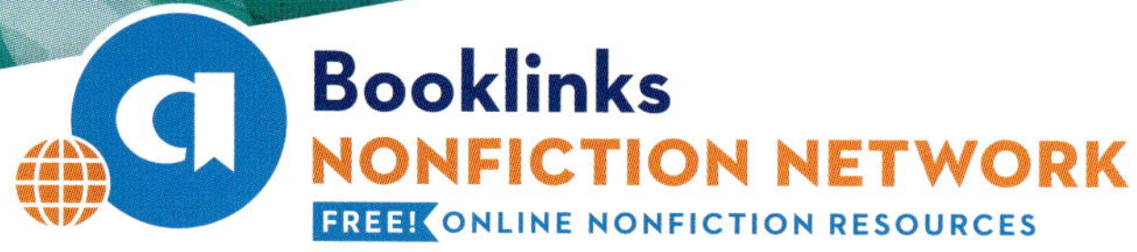

To learn more about *The Monkey King*, please visit **abdobooklinks.com** or scan this QR code. These links are routinely monitored and updated to provide the most current information available.